THE HOW AND WHY WONDER BOOK OF

TREES

Written by ALLEN PATERSON
Illustrated by JOHN BARBER

Acer Nikoense

Pine

Sycamore

Maple

Willow

Plane

Magnolia

TRANSWORLD PUBLISHERS · LONDON

Oak

Palm (coconut)

Introduction

Men have always been fascinated by trees; in early times certain types of trees or certain groves were thought to be the home of the Gods or indeed worthy of worship themselves. This sort of reverence still occurs in remote parts of the world.

Such superstition is not now a part of our modern world but the fascination remains. We are bound to be impressed by realising that trees are the biggest and oldest of living things. Who would not be amazed at the great Californian redwoods, some of which were old 1000 years before Columbus discovered America, or at some of the Australian eucalyptus which are taller than the cross on the dome of St. Paul's Cathedral in London?

When we realise, too, that trees are the providers of so many of man's needs from timber for building and fuel to fruit and rubber and cocoa and chewing-gum. Trees contribute also to the conservation of the Earth's surface as a fertile, food producing area; without them ground can become arid desert and even climate can change. Perhaps then it is not surprising that primitive man found them holy. It is necessary for all of us in the twentieth century to protect trees at all times and plant more when possible; not, of course, for ourselves but for posterity.

Originally published in Great Britain
by Transworld Publishers Ltd.

PRINTING HISTORY
Transworld Edition Published 1974
Copyright © 1974 Transworld Publishers Ltd.
All rights reserved.
The How and Why Wonder Book Series is originated
and published in the U.S.A. by Grosset and Dunlap Inc.,
a National General Company.
Published by Transworld Publishers Ltd., 57/59 Uxbridge Road, Ealing, London W.5.
Printed by Purnell & Sons Ltd., Paulton (Somerset) and London.

Contents

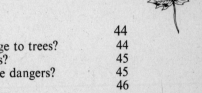

Maritime Pine

Date Palm

4

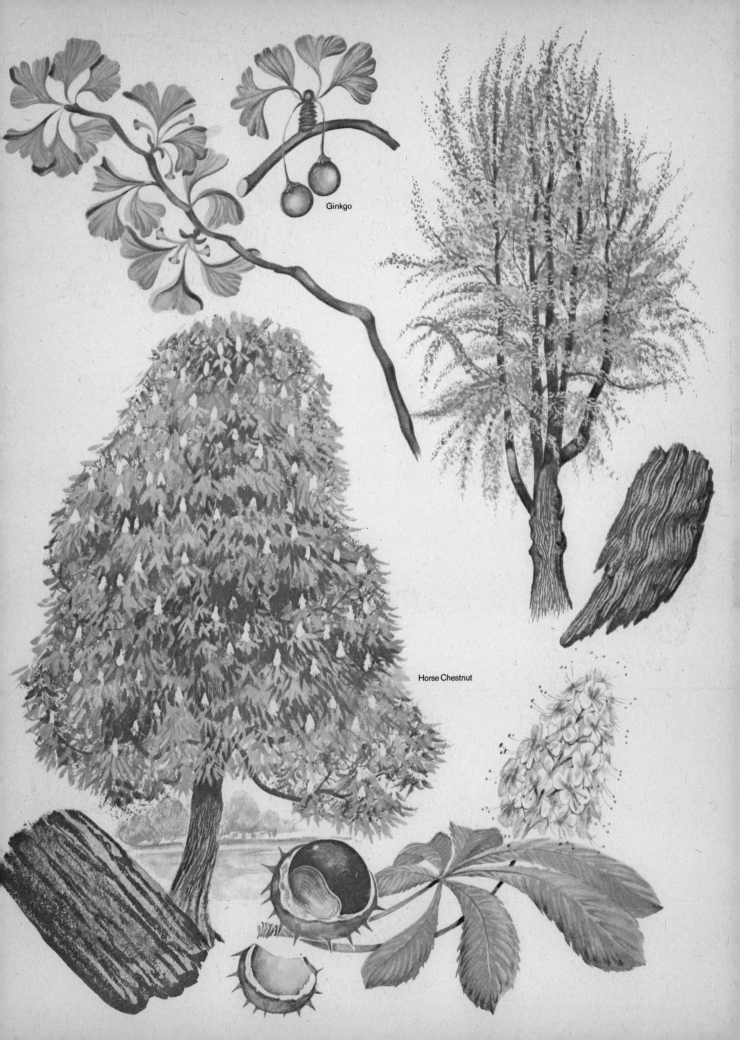

Ginkgo

Horse Chestnut

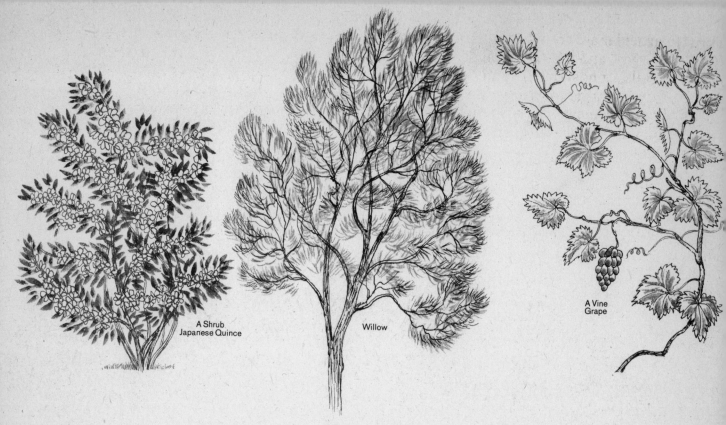

A Shrub
Japanese Quince

Willow

A Vine
Grape

The Willow is a *tree*.

What is a Tree?

What is a tree? Everybody knows, or thinks they know, a tree when they see one, although it is not quite as simple as that. We hear about tree-ferns, tree-peonies, tree-tomatoes or talk of banana trees and rose trees, but none of these are really trees. A tree is a plant which in living for a number, often a very large number, of years produces a thick woody stem or trunk from which a leafy head develops. Eventually it flowers and produces seeds in order to reproduce itself. Thus a tree could be quite small in stature—an old mountain ash growing three feet high in a cleft of rock is as much a tree as one fifty feet high growing in rich soil. For centuries in Japan a technique of artificially dwarfing trees, called Bonsai, has been perfected. Here the typical shape of forest trees can be obtained in a small pot and they are considered to be of great value.

How do trees grow? Trees are still plants however big they become. This means they need certain foods for growth and, depending on where each type or species comes from in the world, certain conditions for growth. They are also living things so that firstly they need air. This is of course always available but it must be remembered that roots need it too. Sunlight and warmth, at least for part of the year, are needed; water, though in different quantities for different species, is essential; and lastly, plant foods. Three elements in particular are required: nitrogen, which is a gas, and the chemical salts of two metals, phosphorus and potassium. Tiny quantities of many other so-called Trace Elements such as sulphur, calcium and magnesium are also vital for plant growth.

The short answer is of course 'the soil'.

Where do plant foods come from? It is, however, necessary, in explaining how trees grow, to discover something about the soil from which they spring. From the earliest times the rocky materials

Dwarfed Pine Tree (Bonsai)

Banyan Tree

Strangler Fig

Odd plants—but still trees.

that make up this planet Earth have been subject to weathering. All rocks, from the extremely hard granite to soft chalk, are worn away by the forces of water and wind, heat and cold and by chemical action. Only the speed of weathering varies; glaciation is a dramatic form of weathering, the gradual dissolving of limestone by the effects of water and carbon dioxide in the air until caves are formed is a much slower process. But both have a product: smaller and smaller pieces of rock which are the basis of soil.

Depending upon the origins of the type of rocks that were broken down the soils **What is soil made up of?** that develop differ in chemical content and physical behaviour. Some hold water well and are thus likely to support good plant growth; other types may be less effective. And in direct proportion as a developing soil supports simple, then bigger, plants and so in turn as these, and the bodies of animals of all sizes that feed upon them, decay so that soil becomes richer and

7

able to support even greater plant growth. So the basic inorganic chemicals of a soil are augmented by *humus* which is composed of the residues of decayed organic matter. When we add manure or compost to a garden soil we are increasing the humus content in order to obtain bigger crops.

The processes of weathering which

How do plants obtain their food from the soil?

began thousands of millions of years ago on the newly formed rocks continues today in the soil and as it does so chemicals are released from the inorganic soil particles and from the organic humus as it is further broken down by bacteria. These chemicals are dissolved in the soil water which drains away into streams and rivers and eventually into the sea. Before it does so, however, much is taken up by plants and the bigger the plant, as in the case of trees which are the biggest plants, the more that is taken up.

Any normal flowering plant that you

How do trees obtain their food from the soil?

pull up clearly has roots. These roots have two main roles. One is to anchor the plant in its position and to try to make sure it does not blow over or get washed away in a storm, the other is to obtain for its nutrition and growth the plant foods it needs. The roots can only take up these foods in solution from the soil water and thus in order to get enough food far more water than is actually needed has to be taken up. This surplus subsequently has to be got rid of. In dry countries, in particular, trees have to search great areas for the water and plant foods they require. Anywhere it is probably true that the roots spread under the ground and cover as great an area as can be seen of branches and leaves in the air above.

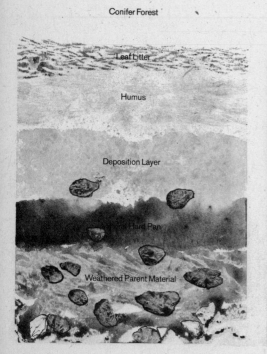

Conifer Forest

Leaf Litter

Humus

Deposition Layer

Hard Pan

Weathered Parent Material

Temperate Grassland

Humus + Mixed Parent Material

Salt Deposits

Weathered Parent Material

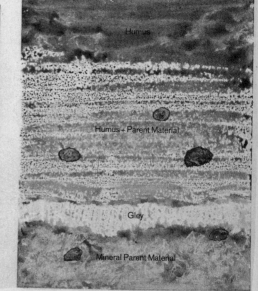

Deciduous Forest

Leaf Litter

Humus

Humus + Parent Material

Gley

Mineral Parent Material

Different types of soil.

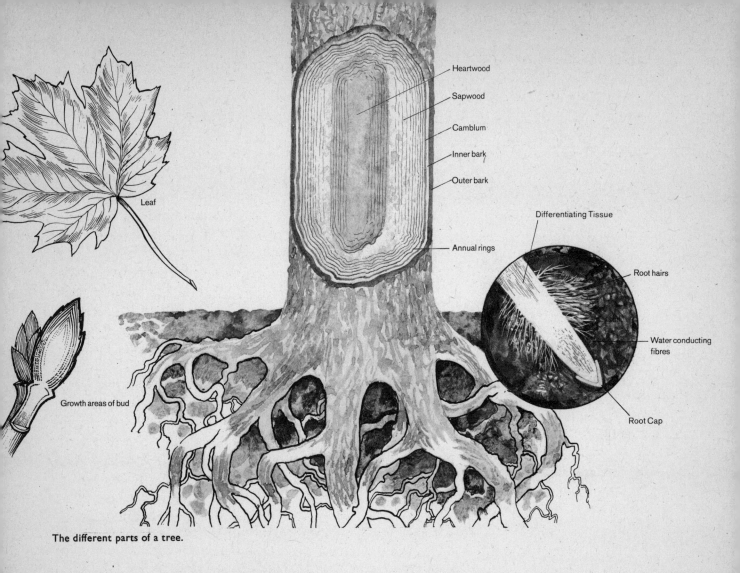

Leaf

Growth areas of bud

Heartwood

Sapwood

Camblum

Inner bark

Outer bark

Annual rings

Differentiating Tissue

Root hairs

Water conducting fibres

Root Cap

The different parts of a tree.

The Parts of Trees

It is clear that each part of a tree has a specific role to perform, or job to do. All parts, the roots, trunk, branches, twigs, leaves, flowers and fruits, have been carefully adapted to fulfil their function with the greatest success. For upon their success depends the ability of any species of tree to survive the intense competition in a forest or jungle for the air, light, water and food that every plant needs. Trees whose parts have not been perfectly adapted to their environment or which have been unable to adapt to changing environmental conditions have become extinct. Some of these are mentioned later. From all climatic conditions all over the world the vast range of trees is a product of this intense search to be most successful in any given habitat, be it within the Arctic Circle or at sea level on the Equator. All the living parts of a tree are made up of millions of cells, just as all parts of a human body are composed of cells. Similarly, these in turn have specific jobs to do such as the transference of food up or down plants. Although the basic body cells of a tree exist in all its parts specialised cells occur in the leaves, flowers and other organs where specialised jobs have to be done.

9

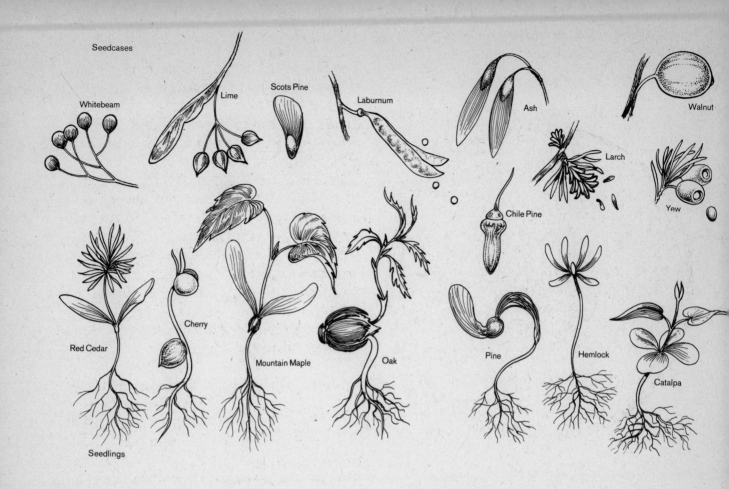

Seedcases

Whitebeam · Lime · Scots Pine · Laburnum · Ash · Walnut · Larch · Yew · Chile Pine

Red Cedar · Cherry · Mountain Maple · Oak · Pine · Hemlock · Catalpa

Seedlings

Unless a tree is able to get itself

Why do trees have a trunk? above or at least level with its competitors in the intense search for the necessities of life it will die. Plants which have been unable to develop a trunk have had to adapt themselves in other ways, to climb, perhaps, like a vine, to grow high on the branches of existing trees like some ferns and orchids or merely to be able to live in shade. Some plants go through their life cycle so quickly that they have not developed any particular mechanism for making the most of their habitat except that of speed in utilising a sudden gap in the canopy above through the fall of a forest giant. Trees on the other hand have gone to the other extreme. In developing a great central stem which in turn supports a huge head of branches and leaves a tree has re-

nounced the possibility of quick returns. It may be twenty or thirty years or even more before the tree, which has spent all this time in building up its vegetative body, is mature enough to flower and fruit and thus to reproduce its species.

Although some trees can reproduce

How do trees reproduce? naturally through suckers coming up from the roots, like the English Elm, and many others may be vegetatively propagated artificially in various ways as are special varieties of apples or oranges or rubber trees, most trees reproduce by seeds. The seeds may be so tiny that as with willows and poplars they are blown around in the air or like the Coco de Mer of the Seychelles which is as big as two rugby balls joined together side by side. But every viable seed, if it

10

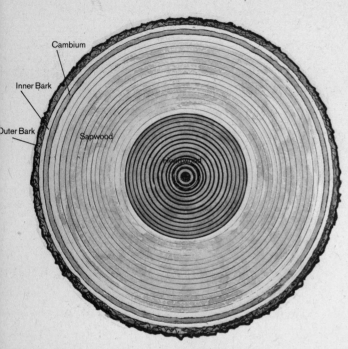

Cross-section of a tree-trunk showing the annual rings.

into the veins of the leaves. Each year as growth begins in the spring a cylinder of cells just inside the skin starts to divide. This cylinder is called the *cambium*. On its inside it makes wood cells or *xylem*; on its outside it makes bast cells or *phloem*. It also has to add to its own girth because the new cells inside the stem push the rest outwards. In temperate climates such as Britain, North America or New Zealand there are two noticeable periods of cell division growth; the rapid spring period when the new cells are large and a summer period when they are smaller with thicker walls.

As the young trunk gets older the

What is the bark? very outside protective layer of cells cannot keep up with all the pressures from inside and cracks appear. These are filled up by a corky growth to prevent diseases getting into the tree. The fissured and corky outside thus becomes the bark; sometimes it is so thick and spongy as to be able to be taken off and used by man. The Cork Oak of the Mediterranean is the most famous example, and is cropped again and again. Bark is also used to make birch-bark canoes in Canada and is a provider of tanning materials but here trees have to be cut down to obtain the bark.

Each year the cambium cells continue to divide, adding a further layer of wood cells on the inside. The earliest wood cells, after a few years, become tightly compressed and die. They are, however, still of great value to the tree as they provide the strength which supports the canopy of branches and leaves above. Only the relatively thin layer, beneath the bark and outside of the wood, is truly alive, through which all the movement of foods and water pass up and down the tree.

finds a suitable site for germination, will start to grow. Usually a root emerges from the seed coat first and grows downwards. It is followed by a tiny shoot which grows upwards towards the light. It is this shoot that ultimately, unless it is eaten off by a rabbit or is burnt in a fire, develops into the enormous column of wood that we call the tree-trunk.

As the shoot grows upward, producing leaves as it goes,

What makes a tree-trunk possible? it also thickens in girth. All this growth is made possible by the constant division of the different sorts of cells in the young stem. Those that are particularly important in causing trunk development are the food conducting tissues that start as *vascular bundles*. These are groups of cells which later join into rings that run up the stem

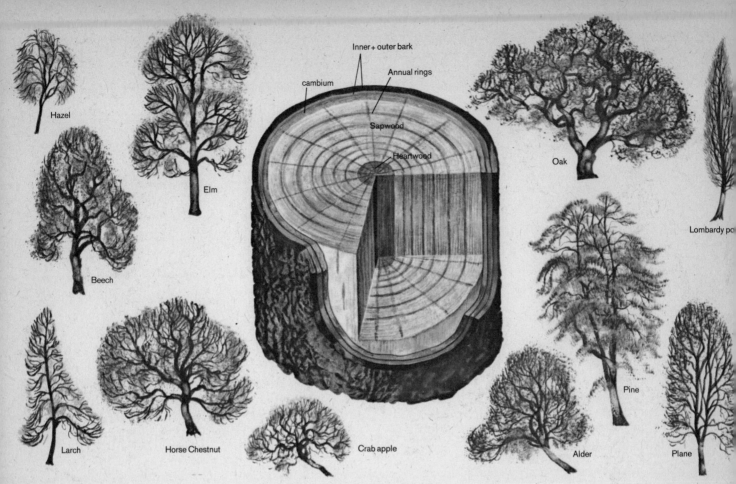

Tree trunks and branches.

Labels on the diagram: Inner + outer bark, Annual rings, cambium, Sapwood, Heartwood

Tree labels: Hazel, Elm, Beech, Larch, Horse Chestnut, Crab apple, Oak, Lombardy po[plar], Pine, Alder, Plane

How old is a tree? If a tree is cut down it is possible to count the number of layers of cells that have been laid down in the building up of the trunk. These are annual rings. Over 3,500 rings have been counted in the oldest living trees known. These are specimens of the Bristlecone Pines in California and Arizona. Fortunately it is not necessary to cut down a tree to discover its age. A drill has been perfected which having bored into the trunk can bring out a thin 'tube' of wood on which it is possible to count the rings. The hole left soon heals over.

Why do trees have branches? Most trees develop a trunk which gets above the surrounding herbage and then divides again and again to make up a great crowd of branches, branchlets and twigs. Thus some tropical trees need to reach two hundred feet before they divide; in English parkland Oaks may divide at only a few feet above the ground and grow even wider than they do high. Typically fir-trees and many other conifers keep a central trunk right to the tip of the tree. This is known as *apical dominance*. The branches are composed of the same tissues as the trunk and, depending upon their age, will structurally be like the trunk was at that age. Usually a one-year-old twig will be like the tree was in its first year after the seed germinated. The branches, then, develop as high and as widespreading as possible so that the leaf canopy is exposed to the maximum amount of light.

12

zel

Hawthorn

Japanese Maple

Yew

Apple

Willow

Oak

Horse Chestnut

Maple

Holly

Laburnum

Bay

Leaves grow in many different shapes and sizes. This selection shows just a few.

In many ways the leaves are the most vital part of a tree; on the other hand they could not do their job if the roots and trunk and branches and twigs didn't bring them to the position where they can begin to work efficiently. No speck of light is wasted; if you get under a fully grown tree in full summer and look up you will see how each leaf is placed to get as much light as it can. It has been said that leaves are the lungs of plants. But this is an understatement; they are far more than that. At the most simple it is through the leaves that the exchange of gases, inevitable in any living organism, takes place. It is also through the leaves that the most vital organic process takes place which makes life as we know it on this

What function does the leaves serve?

planet possible at all. This is *photosynthesis*.

All green plants have the capability of making complicated organic substances, sugars and starches, from simple inorganic chemicals. Most of the cells in the leaves and young and still green stems possess bodies known as *chloroplasts* in which is contained a green material called *chlorophyll*. This acts as a chemical catalyst which facilitates, but does not itself become changed in, the conversion of carbon dioxide from the air and water from the roots, in the presence of sunlight, into sugars. This is the vital process called *photosynthesis* and means, literally, 'building up in the presence of light'.

Why are leaves green?

13

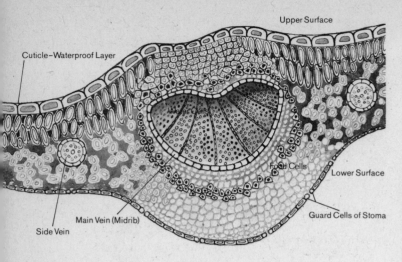

Upper Surface

Cuticle–Waterproof Layer

Palisade Cells

Food Cells

Lower Surface

Main Vein (Midrib)

Side Vein

Guard Cells of Stoma

A cross-section of a leaf to show its cell structure.

How do the gases get in and out?

If an exchange of gases is to be possible they must be able to move in and out of the plant easily. This is done through countless tiny pores, called *stomata*, on the underside of each leaf (they are not on the upper surface excepting, for example, the water-lily, for obvious reasons). Each stoma can be opened and closed depending upon conditions but usually they are open during most of the day and some of the night. During the day-time carbon-dioxide is taken in for photosynthetic sugar-making and oxygen as a by-product is given off. Water vapour is also let out because, it will be remembered, in most areas much more moisture than is needed is brought up by the roots in the process of collecting plant foods from the soil water.

At night the photosynthesis has to stop because there is no light, but respiration, which uses oxygen and gives off carbon dioxide (as do our exhaling lungs), continues, so stomata may stay open. However, in periods of very drying winds or in times of drought the plant tries to keep them shut to prevent being dried out. If this occurs it will go limp and may well die.

Why do leaves of trees differ so much in size and shape?

It must be said again that each tree is as nearly ideally adapted to its habitat as possible. Thus, remembering their function, leaves can tell us a lot about the place and climate from which any species comes. We can expect large leaves on trees from semi-shaded areas where light is at a premium, but also where damage from wind is not likely. Many tropical forest trees are like this. Where growth occurs in a seasonal pattern the leaves again reflect this. In areas with a Mediterranean type of climate, for example, leaves are typically small and leathery or they may be grey and hairy. Both types help the plant to conserve moisture in the hot, dry summers. In the winter it is moist and still reasonably mild so the leaves can continue to do their work and the plant continues to grow.

In much colder climates trees become almost completely dormant in the winter. Here two types of leaf pattern are possible. Either they must be able to resist extreme cold as do the conifers which cover so much of the northern areas of America, Europe and Asia or they must develop some other method of dealing successfully with the situation.

An evergreen.

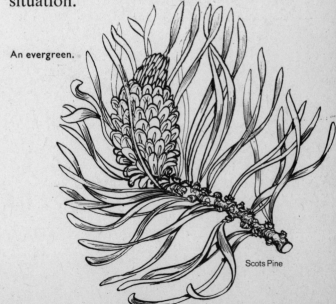

Scots Pine

This has been done by one very large group of trees

Why do some trees lose their leaves in autumn?

that are described as being *deciduous*, as distinct from being *evergreen* like the Mediterranean and tropical forest trees and the vast majority of conifers. Deciduous trees emerge from their winter dormancy by expanding their overwintering buds from which emerge new leaves and the shoot which will make that season's extension growth. On the shoot further leaves, and possibly flowers, develop. Throughout the late spring, summer and early autumn these leaves perform their vital functions but as it becomes colder it is less easy for them to do so. Two processes then begin; where the leaf-stalk joins the twig a thin layer of cork, like that behind the bark, is laid down. At the same time the twig brings back from the leaf all it can of useful foods and chemicals so that by the time the cork layer is fully formed and the leaf is cut off from the twig little of value remains. The wind can then blow the leaves off. Left behind is a scar with a pattern of dots; these are where the veins joined the vascular bundles of the twig. Thus what could be considered an incredibly wasteful method of replacing the leaf canopy annually is made much less so. The combination of changes in the chemical constituents of the leaf and rapid changes in climate and the onset of frost cause the leaves, particularly in some species and some seasons, to develop the most striking colours of yellow, red and orange. In North America the autumn is always called the Fall.

The incredible displays of autumn leaf colours are easily

Why are some leaves never green?

explained. They are a temporary situation and refer to leaves that are dead or dying. But some trees have coloured leaves all the year round. In temperate countries there are purple leaved trees, such as Copper Beech or Purple Sycamore, which are planted for their ornamental effect. Tropical Crotons are even brighter. Here the colour is caused by a pigment which masks the chlorophyll-green of the leaves though making them no less effective in their work. Some trees, however, have white or gold blotches or edges to their leaves. These are said to be *variegated*; although these forms occur naturally they would not normally survive in the wild. The green photosynthetic areas are reduced and the tree is less strong. But they are often very attractive so one may see such types in gardens or parks.

How leaves fall in autumn.

Elm Leaf Before Sealing Off

All vital elements withdrawn
Leaf shrivels as sealing off takes place

Sealing off completed.
Leaf falls to ground
to aid new growth

Tree flowers.

Do trees flower as do other plants?

Obviously any true seed-producing plant whether it grows three inches high or three hundred feet high must produce flowers. Certainly on a wide range of trees, especially the conifers, the flowers are not easily apparent because they may not have colourful petals. But many trees, particularly in tropical countries, have splendid displays of flowers in all colours. Blue Jacarandas and scarlet Flamboyants are examples. In cooler climates Magnolias and Horse-chestnuts are spectacular flowering trees which are frequently planted because of this.

What are the flowers for?

From the human point of view we are apt to regard the flowers just as something attractive to look at. But they are to the tree of far greater importance as the inevitable preliminary to seed production and thus the reproduction of the tree. Most flowers contain both the male (stamens) and female (stigma and ovary) reproductive parts within the same set of petals. Such trees are described as being hermaphrodite; others, however, such as hazel-nut, have separate male and female flowers (the male flowers are the long 'lambs' tails' or catkins we see in early spring)

16

and a further group have separate male and female plants. Thus the male holly tree will never have berries.

The petals, with the frequent addition of nectar and a scent, attract insects or in the tropics sometimes humming birds. In collecting the nectar these creatures transfer pollen from the stamens to the stigma and from flower to flower. Usually only pollen from the same species is acceptable to any stigma. The pollen grains grow down into the ovary and cause the seeds to develop. This is called fertilization.

Not all trees depend upon bees

How are trees without petals pollinated?

or moths or humming birds for pollination. Many produce so much pollen that a less definite method suffices. Here the pollen is carried about by the wind and long feathery stigmas of the female flowers catch it, after which the process is the same.

The vital process of reproduction is

What happens after fertilization?

only half completed by the seeds developing in the ovary of the female part of the flower. The next problem for a tree is to evolve a method of distributing ripe seeds over as wide an area as possible. Each habitat provides problems which have had to be overcome. It is of little use in a forest if all seeds from a tree just fall to the ground underneath the parent plant. They may germinate but it is likely to be too dark for them to reach the light and they will die when still young. Thus a wide range of seed dispersal mechanisms has evolved. Use of the wind is of great importance; most cypress seeds are very small and light and can blow some distance; sycamore has wings on a pair of seeds which gives a helicopter effect; willows and poplars have tiny seeds embedded in downy fluff. Other trees use animals to help seed dispersal. You may have

Horse Chestnut

Flower

Ovary

Style

Stamens

Seed Case

An hermaphrodite flower.

Hazel

Male Flowers

Female Flower

Seed Case

Separate male and female flowers on the same tree.

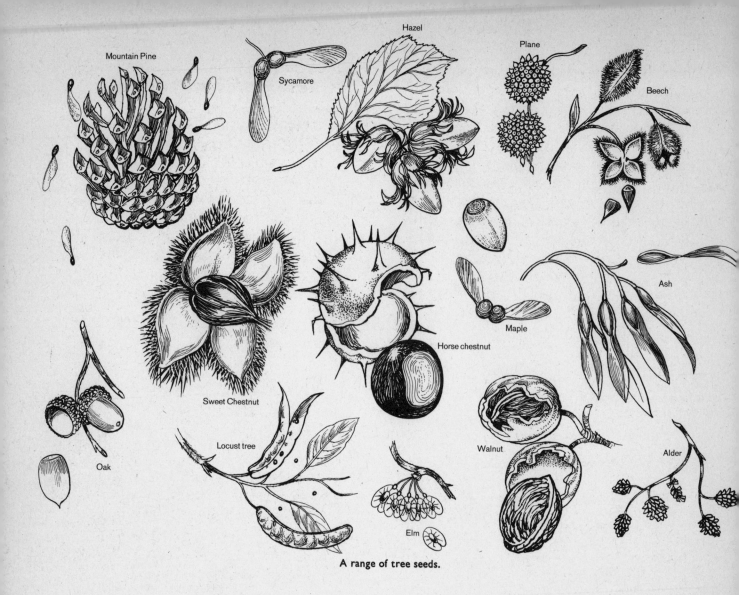

A range of tree seeds.

Labels: Mountain Pine, Sycamore, Hazel, Plane, Beech, Ash, Maple, Horse chestnut, Sweet Chestnut, Locust tree, Oak, Walnut, Elm, Alder

seen squirrels collecting and carrying off and burying nuts or acorns for later use. Fortunately for the nut tree or oak tree, squirrels' memories are not good and so not only are the seeds distributed but they are also planted and not all are found again.

Birds too are the most enormous help and most of the fleshy fruits have been developed as a food attraction. Yew or hawthorn berries are eaten whole but the seed itself passes through the animals' systems to emerge unharmed and is conveniently deposited with a small dash of fertilizer. This explains why a hedge so quickly develops along the line of a wire fence.

Are there any unusual methods of seed dispersal?

In some habitats very specific methods of seed dispersal have been developed. Two good tropical examples can be given. Most seeds quickly become infertile in water and especially in salt water. But coconut palms often overhang the sea. Their seeds, the coco-nuts themselves, may drop into the water but they are excellently protected by the thick fibrous outer coats (which we never see on coco-nuts bought in a shop). They are also very buoyant and the nuts can float around the tropical sea for months before being washed up

18

on a beach to germinate in the sand.

Mangroves, which actually grow in sea water, are even more extraordinary. Here the seeds are not big and buoyant. Anyway, merely floating to the shore would not help; they need to get to the muddy bottom below several feet of water. Here the seed starts to germinate on the parent tree and produces, as all seeds do, its first root. This is hard and like a torpedo. When it is about three inches long the whole thing drops from the tree and dives into the water to stick in the mud beneath. It can then start to send up a shoot above water.

Thus each tree has its own methods of growing, flowering and fruiting which are the most effective for its own particular conditions of life. These are worth observing. Without perfect adaptation to an environment no organism can successfully continue. This is why many trees which once existed are no longer to be found and why some, once very common, are now very rare.

The Diversity of Trees

As can be guessed from the previous section on seed dispersal, some trees grow in extraordinary situations. So long as the five main conditions needed for plant growth exist—water, light, air, warmth and food—and are met in sufficient quantities, trees will grow. In real desert conditions no plant growth is of course possible, but on the edges of the arid zones some trees especially adapted to drought will grow, as date palms, for example, in the Sahara do at any spot

Do trees grow everywhere?

where more moisture is present. Sometimes another factor has to be considered. For instance, extreme exposure to wind can be limiting and in coastal regions contorted specimens are seen leaning and growing away from the prevailing gales. When wind exposure is combined with cold as on high mountains then tree growth becomes impossible. In mountain ranges a 'tree-line' is noticeable above which only small shrubs and herbaceous plants succeed. Eventually conditions become so bad that no plant will grow and of course snow is continually present above certain heights.

Tree growth is prevented by wind and cold working together and so the altitude of the tree-line will differ considerably. Thus the nearer the equator one goes the higher up mountains trees will grow. In Scotland, for instance, the tree-line is naturally at about 3,000 feet, whilst in parts of

Is the tree-line constant throughout the world?

Date palms.

the Himalayas or the mountains of monsoon Africa it is above three times that. And local conditions, of sheltered valleys and (in the northern hemisphere) southern slopes, will affect things.

Although the tree-line in Scotland would be normally around 3,000 feet, man's pressure on trees has been so great as to virtually change the landscape. In early times the forests of Birch and Scots Pine on the higher slopes and Oak, Ash and Alder lower down were the source of all fuel and building materials. Later, especially from the eighteenth century, the policy of great landowners was to clear the ground for profitable sheep farming and for deer 'forests'. Not only was much of the Highlands deforested, it was also depopulated and large numbers of highlanders emigrated to the New World. The words 'deer forest' are still used for areas where herds of red deer are carefully conserved for stalking, but trees hardly exist at all. In some areas trees are returning to the Highlands and these are usually exotic species of conifers planted for their timber.

Why are there no trees at all on most Scottish mountains?

The previous sections begin to answer this question. Over the millions of years of evolutionary time since the Earth's crust cooled and the seas and continents became delineated (although not as we now know them) small plants and trees evolved. Those that succeeded best were the ones that were able to adapt most effectively to their habitats. As climate changed and changed again through mountain-making earth movements, in a few places where change

Why is there such a diversity of trees?

was least, trees survived unaltered. Elsewhere many types died out completely, like the dinosaurs of the animal kingdom, because they could not adapt to the new conditions. Meanwhile, in response to these conditions, new species evolved more suited to them. This description is, of course, a great oversimplification of the complicated and continuous process of evolution but it does indicate how plants (and indeed all living organisms) have needed to adapt continually if their species are to survive. It should also be remembered that evolution is still occurring but that changes are so minute in a man's lifetime that individually we are barely conscious of it.

It is hardly to be expected that many trees which developed hundreds of

What do we know of the early trees?

Primitive trees in a prehistoric forest.

20

millions of years ago have been able to survive through all the changes that have occurred since then. Most of our knowledge, then, comes from fossil records. Sometimes leaves, flowers, twigs or even whole trunks have been preserved in rock layers so perfectly that they are easily recognised by experts.

Some of the best remains are in coal measures. Coal is composed entirely of plant residues of great tropical forests which existed some 250,000,000 years ago in many, now temperate, parts of the world. Almost all of those trees are now extinct, though their remains show many of them to have been giant ancestors of some existing primitive plants such as horsetails and club-mosses. These are non-flowering but spore-bearing plants related to ferns. A few coal-age trees amazingly do still exist. One is Ginkgo, sometimes called 'Maidenhair Tree' because of its leaves' likeness to maidenhair fern. This tall tree, although once common on the Earth, survived only in China from whence seeds were collected by early Western travellers and it is now quite a common ornamental tree in Western Europe and the U.S.A. Another is even more remarkable; this is Metasequoia, the Dawn Redwood, another deciduous conifer. Although it had been known by its fossils for a long time it was always presumed extinct until a small grove of it was discovered in 1945 in N.W. China. Seeds reached the West in 1948 and now Metasequoia trees over fifty feet high are growing in many parks and gardens. From an evolutionary point of view this is as remarkable as if people were able to keep coelacanths in home aquaria!

Fossil remains of leaves have been found preserved in rock layers.

Ginkgo

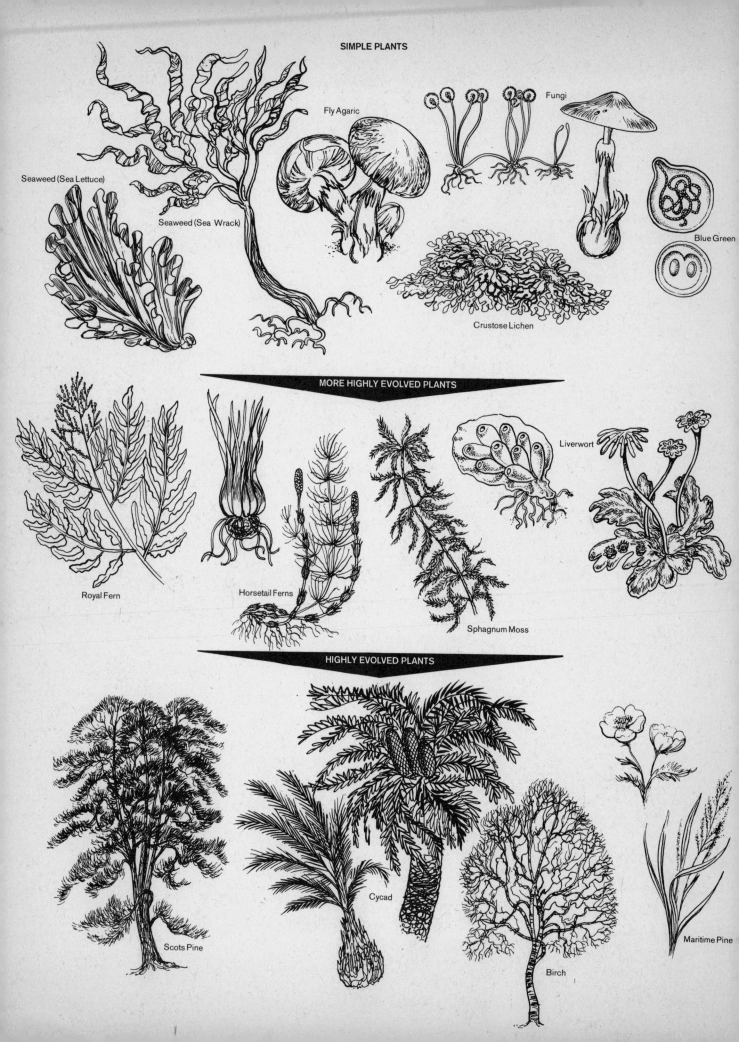

SIMPLE PLANTS

Seaweed (Sea Lettuce)

Seaweed (Sea Wrack)

Fly Agaric

Fungi

Blue Green

Crustose Lichen

MORE HIGHLY EVOLVED PLANTS

Royal Fern

Horsetail Ferns

Sphagnum Moss

Liverwort

HIGHLY EVOLVED PLANTS

Scots Pine

Cycad

Birch

Maritime Pine

Any system of classification to some extent depends **What are the main types of living trees?** upon who is doing it and for what reason. Thus botanists and foresters will have different descriptions and names for trees, which is apt to be confusing.

The botanist is concerned with relationships between trees and how they grow naturally while the forester is concerned with improving on nature and with economic uses of the timbers or the other products of the trees. It is perhaps wise to look first through the botanist's eyes. Plants are divided into groups depending on their complexity and thus their degree of evolution.

It can be seen from the table that only the seed-bearing plants have been able to develop the tissues which make trunks and branches and flowers and seeds possible. The real question therefore is how to sort out the range of trees in these groups.

The most primitive group of trees, the cycads, is only a small one; most have become extinct. They are all from tropical or sub-tropical areas and mainly from the Southern hemisphere. They look rather like small palms with long spiky leaves but whereas palms have heads of flowers cycads produce big cones in the centre of the top circle of leaves and these eventually contain the seeds. Though vastly bigger, the cones are more like those of horsetails than pine-cones which indicates their intermediate relationship between those two groups. In temperate countries one is likely to see cycads in greenhouses in Botanic Gardens; even in their native habitats they are not common and few have any economic use to man.

Silhouettes of conifers.

A cone of a cycad.

The next group of trees, still rather primitive, are **Are the conifers easy to recognise?** much better known but because of their numbers it is easy to over-generalise about them and thus make identification more, not less, difficult. Coniferous trees are of enormous importance both to the botanist and the forester. The great forests of Canada, of Northern Europe and Russia and of mountainous areas in many parts of the world are made up

The leaves and fruits of conifers.

of them. Northern Hemisphere species also have their counterparts in Chile and in Australia and New Zealand. When we see a 'fir-cone' we know it has come from a conifer. But which? Cones can, especially if still on the tree, help with identification: for instance spruce cones hang downwards; those of true firs stand up on the branches; so do cedar cones but these drop scale by scale not whole; pine-cones have usually large scales; cypress cones are round; those of false cypresses are tiny—no bigger than a pea and so on. A few conifers do not even produce their seeds in recognisable cones. Yew has small red fleshy fruits with a poisonous seed, Ginkgo has fruits like a yellow plum—but these smell so unpleasant that no one is likely to eat them.

The leaves also help the diagnosis. We expect conifers to be evergreen but there are exceptions; larch is a common deciduous one and the primitive Ginkgo and Dawn Redwood too both lose their leaves in winter. Mostly, however, the leaves are evergreen, very narrow and up to six inches in length. If the leaves are long and in bunches of up to five, you are probably looking at a pine and the number of 'needles' will help to tell which of the seventy existing species you have found. If you are in its natural habitat this will also help to tell you which species you have found; the Mexican pines are not likely to be growing on an Alpine slope in Switzerland. But it is just for this

24

Swamp Cypress

Ginkgo

Yew

Sequoia

Chile Pine
(Monkey Puzzle)

reason that identification in parks and gardens is difficult because the trees intentionally planted by man have been brought together from many parts of the world.

Although the long narrow pine or fir leaf is common, another group of conifers has small

Are pine needles the only sort of conifer leaf?

wedge shaped leaves that overlap each other like scales on an armadillo's tail. These are the cypresses. One of the sequoias and some of its relations also have them. The true cypresses are trees of warm climates and are only marginally hardy in Britain; they are seen typically as narrow spikes of dark green on dry Mediterranean hillsides.

The false cypresses are all from the New World as are the Sequoias or Redwoods. Although these are clearly conifers they are the biggest trees that grow; indeed the biggest of all living things on this planet.

The cones produce seeds as can be seen if any ripe pine-cone is placed on a radiator or in a

Do conifers have flowers?

gentle oven. The scales open and the winged seeds shake out. And if there are seeds they must have been preceded by flowers. But conifers are primitive plants and sophisticated pollinating mechanisms with attractive petals and scents to attract insects have not been evolved.

25

Separate male and female cones develop on the branches, sometimes, as with Yew, on separate trees. Usually the male cones are like small catkins and produce huge quantities of dust-like pollen some of which blows onto the receptive areas of the young female cones and fertilization occurs. These are the cones which grow.

What are the trees in the higher-plant groups?

The trees in the higher-plant groups are the so-called 'b r o a d l e a v e d hardwoods' to distinguish them from the 'softwoods' or conifers. This is a confusing and often nonsensical division; some coniferous woods such as Yew are extremely hard while some 'hardwoods' like Poplar and especially Balsa are very soft indeed. It is safer to call these the higher seed-bearing trees, the word 'higher' referring of course to their evolutionary position not to the height they grow! And not all, unfortunately, have broad leaves. All this indicates the difficulty of classifying plants which exist in such a wealth of differing types.

Silhouettes of English trees—broad-leaved hardwoods.

Elm   Oak   Sweet Chestnut   Wych Elm

A tropical forest.

Aroid   Strawberry Fig   Epiphyte   Fungi   Butress Roots

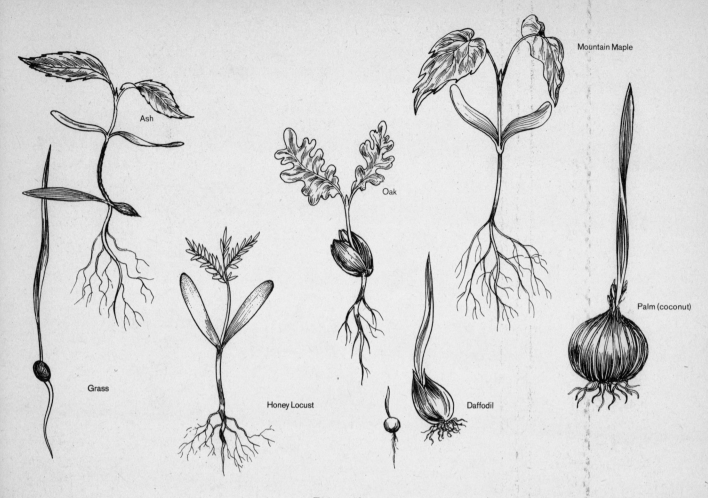

Tree seedlings.

Within the enormous range two main sections can be separated.

How can the higher seed bearing trees be identified?

These are called *dicotyledons* and *monocotyledons*. A cotyledon is a seed leaf. If you sow a grass seed or a coconut (which is itself a seed) a single leaf will first emerge; these are monocotyledons. If you sow a lettuce or a sycamore seed two seedleaves will appear; these belong to the other category. 'Monocot' trees are much less common and are mainly tropical, but they include the vastly important range of palms. Almost all the other trees we know are 'dicots' and in their different botanical families inhabit all corners of the Earth, from the steaming equatorial jungles to birch woods inside the Arctic Circle. Here are the nut-trees, fruit-trees, very many timber-trees without which man's life would be made difficult, if not impossible.

There is no reason why coniferous and broadleaved trees should not share the same areas.

Do both groups of trees grow together?

Certainly in cultivation we see pines and cedars growing happily near oaks or tulip-trees. But in the wild each species is so particularly suited to local conditions that it is usual for one tree to be dominant and thus more frequent than others. Such dominance is much less noticeable in tropical forests where a great range of species grows together in a frantic fight for light and air.

The local uses of palms.

Many oak-trees were felled in Elizabethan times to build warships.

Trees and Men

It has been said before that without trees man's life upon this planet would either be impossible or so different that it is difficult to imagine. Trees are so valuable in so many ways. With just one use try to think how you could live without wood for furniture, floors and rafters in houses, wood for making paper, wood for building boats. It certainly is difficult even in the twentieth century when some alternative materials are becoming available. This chapter, therefore, considers what trees give to man.

This question can be answered in several ways; **What are the most valuable timbers?** valuable to whom, in quantity or quality? In primitive societies where temporary huts are built with branches and thatched with leaves it probably doesn't matter much what trees are used. But when buildings are expected to last, or when they are very large, the type matters a lot. This is why in Northern Europe the English Oak has always been of great importance. It is hard, longlasting, not easily attacked by woodworm, and available in large sizes. In ship-building in the sixteenth century in England it was of great importance as the shape of the oak branches was seen to be ideal for 'knees'. But trees which take a hundred and fifty years or so to come to maturity are not quickly replaceable and as early as the 1650's John Evelyn, a friend of Samuel Pepys ('Founder of the British Navy'), was recommending

Walnut was the most sought after wood for furniture during the reigns of William and Mary and Queen Anne.

that woods with ornamental grains—that is the patterns that the annual rings make when tree-trunks are cut longitudinally, tangentially or straight across—should be used. Thus during the reigns of William and Mary and Queen Anne walnut was the most sought after wood and beautiful bureaux and chests of drawers with figured grain may still be seen. In France where sweet chestnut was a common wood it was frequently made up into furniture.

When did foreign woods begin to be used? As the New World began to be opened up during the sixteenth century and ships from Western Europe rounded Cape Horn and others reached India and the Orient via the Cape of Good Hope they brought back valuables of every kind. Gold and silver were always sought but often less exciting but more useful products were carried. Amongst these, rare woods from tropical countries became predominant. The vogue for mahogany, first from Cuba, then Honduras and tropical Central America, was such that from the time its timber was first brought in quantity to Britain in the 1730s little important furniture of anything else was made for towards a hundred and fifty years. And since then, the original forests being worked out, while rich red mahogany is still in demand all over the world, alternative timbers have had to be found with similar characteristics.

Mahogany is not, of course, the only tropical timber of great economic importance. Rosewood especially since about 1800 has been in great demand; teak from tropical Asia and a host of exotic woods with equally exotic names such as kingwood and zebrawood have all been used and brought back to the Old World.

that landowners should *plant*, not merely cut, oaks, for use in the future. It was as well for Nelson's Navy in the Napoleonic wars that many did so. Oak was also the predominant wood used inside houses before the eighteenth century. Visit an Elizabethan mansion and notice how the long refectory tables, the chairs, the cupboards and the dark linenfold panelling and the timbers behind, if you could see them, are all made from this marvellous wood.

Were other woods used for furniture? In the country areas local timbers have always been used; thus simple furniture of beech, elm, yew and imported pine (or deal, as it is often called) was made all over Britain until recent times. But furniture for wealthy people was apt to follow fashion, and fashion decreed

In all parts of the world local timbers have always been of vital importance, firstly to a simple economy and later to a highly developed one. Settlers in the eastern states of North America were delighted to find forests of fine trees suitable for houses and furniture making, for fuel and ship building: Oaks, Maples, Hickories and Tulip-trees. In Canada they found the apparently inexhaustible conifer forests of Lawson's Cypress, Hemlocks, Spruces and Firs and across on the Pacific Ocean side Western Red Cedars and the incredible Redwoods. In Australia the huge range of gum-trees (these are Eucalyptus of which there are over 500 species) between them fulfils almost every role. They are not, as people in Britain often seem to think, just food for Koala bears and producers of oil to use when we have a cold, but fine timber-trees of every sort. Since they grow so quickly many species are grown now in other warm parts of the world and are quite changing the local landscapes.

Are there other important timber-trees?

New Zealand, too, has a fine range of native timbers especially fine hardwooded conifers, species of Podocarpus and Agathis.

Throughout the world, indeed, from the New World to the Orient in North and South Hemispheres man has found a use for almost every tree that grows. A concern of the twentieth century is that his use of trees is greatly outpacing their replacement. An Oak-tree that has taken two hundred years to reach maturity can be cut down in a very few minutes.

Since our most primitive ancestors wandered through the forests picking

What trees are used for food?

berries and nuts (and possibly making some unfortunate mistakes) trees have been a source of food for man. Even in our highly developed industrial society we still enjoy going out to collect hazel-nuts or chestnuts, crab-apples or wild plums from native plants but man is no longer, in most communities, dependent upon wild plants. Wherever man gave up a nomadic life he has farmed and gardened and thus has grown cultivated forms of the wild plants which he found good for food. It would be seen that this crab-apple tree had sweeter fruits or that wild pear larger ones and so these individuals would be selected and propagated from.

Nowadays, the mysteries of reproduction are understood and desirable characteristics of fruits are bred into new varieties. Thus we have the marvellous range of apples, pears, plums and cherries in cool temperate countries. In warmer ones the citrus fruits—oranges, grapefruit, lemons, tangerines—and peaches and figs are grown. And in tropical countries there are mangoes and pawpaws and dozens more besides. All these are the fleshy fruits which were originally designed by the tree to aid dispersal of its seeds and therefore reproduction of its species. In the processes of hybridisation and selection man has sometimes been able to produce trees whose fleshy fruits develop without the usual seeds; for example, seedless oranges and bananas (not *really* a tree) which never have pips. Such plants always have to be reproduced by vegetative means, such as cuttings, grafting or layering.

Some of those trees whose fruits are not fleshy and where the seeds are protected by hard coats are also food for man. These are what we call nuts, and although in Britain they are mainly a pleasant extra at already excessive

Eating

Coconut palm

Thatching

Drinking

Weaving

Harvesting oil palm

The coconut-tree has many uses.

meals at Christmas-time some nuts are of great importance to some societies. It is worth mentioning that brazil-nuts are one of the few commercial fruits that still come mainly from wild trees in the forests of tropical South America.

In the context of the whole world it is probably safe to say that the most important nut is the coco-nut. Not only is it one of the biggest of all nuts but almost all parts of the tree are useful to man. The Coco-nut is an elegant palm-tree growing up to a hundred feet high. Although possibly originally native to South America because the nuts float so well it has become naturalised in all tropical coastal areas of the world and its typical silhouette is a visual part of all such areas. To the inhabitants coco-nut palms are invaluable; the trunk (porcupine-wood) is useful timber, the leaves are used for thatching, sap which pours from cuts made on the young flower spike can be turned into sugar, and when fermented into vinegar or a strong alcoholic drink known as

Which is the most important nut of all?

toddy. The flesh of the green coco-nut is used as a vegetable, the 'milk' inside the young nut as a fresh drink. Rope, matting and brooms are made from the outside layers which protect the nut. And lastly the mature nut flesh is dried to be a world-important source of vegetable fats and oils. All this comes from a tree which will grow in pure sand. Without coco-nuts it is difficult to know how people in many small tropical-sea islands could survive.

Perhaps the most important source of edible and soap making oil is the Oil Palm. This is not unlike a coco-nut palm with its long divided leaves, but the trunk is not smooth and it is seldom so high. Originally a native of western tropical Africa it is now grown commercially in many tropical countries, especially in Malaysia, Indonesia and in the Congo. The oil-bearing fruits are carried in huge bunches of up to 200 at a time, and the tree can produce from 2 to 6 bunches a year. They are harvested, like coco-nuts, by men climbing with a rope round the trunk and themselves.

Are there other uses of tree-fruits?

Both the wood and the fruit of the olive-tree have been used for many centuries.

What is olive oil?
Whereas palms are a relatively new oil producer the need for oil in the oldest civilisations caused animal fats to be used, and in the Mediterranean area the growing of olive-trees. This small, grey-leaved and, when old, incredibly gnarled tree is a typical sight all the way round the 'Middle Sea'; in fact the definition of a Mediterranean climate can be that in which olives will succeed. Their origin is difficult to determine but it seems likely that the Greeks several centuries before Christ distributed olives from their own country in which they were a staple crop, to their colonies overseas in Italy, France and Spain. But references in the Old Testament of the Bible to olives predate the Greeks. In Biblical Israel olive oil was used for anointing the head and body (this is still ritually carried out at coronations of English Kings and Queens) and for fuel in lamps. The oil itself of course is pressed from the ripe fruit.

Why are there two colours of olives?
The whole olive fruit has been a food, rich in food-value, since these early times but except in simple communities olives are now more a part of cookery and for eating with drinks. The black ones have been picked when fully ripe but the green (which are often stuffed with pimentoes) have been harvested before being fully developed. Olive-trees are extremely slow growing and long-lived so it is not likely that owners of olive-groves would cut them down for timber. However, when it becomes available olive-tree wood is hard with a lovely dark grain and is made into bowls and platters and is highly valued for carving.

32

Lemon

Hazel

Pear

Apple

Beech

Walnut

Young grey Squirrel

Sweet Chestnut

& W—TREES—C

nutmeg

cloves

cocoa

Incas with pure rubber made into balls

Spices were so precious that many wars were fought over the islands on which they grew.

Drinks and Spices

Although reference is often made to tea-trees and coffee-trees it is probably more exact to think of these as little more than shrubs. Certainly in cultivation they are not expected to grow a trunk. Cocoa, however, is different, it really makes a tree. Cocoa-trees are native to tropical South America but now more are grown in West Africa than anywhere else. This is a most unusual tree in that its flowers and, therefore, its fruits are produced on the main trunk and not on the young shoots as with most others. Cocoa 'beans' come from big yellow or red pods.

There are three spices that are particularly important, two of which come from the 'Spice Islands' of Indonesia. So rare and expensive were these spices in early days that the ownership of the producing islands was the cause of many wars and skirmishes. Nutmeg and mace—two very different spices—come from the same tree, *Myristica fragrans*. Nutmegs whole or powdered are well known. When they are harvested the fleshy exterior of the fruit is thrown away but a netted covering of the hard nutmeg is kept and dried. This is mace, which is used in savoury dishes. Not all the spices are from fruits. Cinnamon, a sixty feet high tree from Ceylon, has aromatic bark. Commercially this is obtained from young branches and so that these

Tapping rubber

Some of the things that are made from rubber.

Early explorers were fascinated by this tree sap which made such bouncing balls and brought some of this basic rubber or latex back to Europe. It soon became known that latex could waterproof cloth and make rubber boots but in heat it became sticky and when cold went rock hard so it was not until the vulcanisation process was invented by Charles Goodyear in the U.S.A. in 1839 that rubber could be used without its behaving in this manner and then its possibilities started to be understood. Imagine now transport in the late twentieth century without rubber; almost everything runs on wheels and all have rubber tyres; even the skirt round a wheel-less hovercraft can be of rubber. Latex as produced by the rubber tree is not truly sap but is a by-product of growth which serves, like resins in other trees, to heal wounds.

Latex is a milky liquid which can be obtained from wounding the stem or leaves of

How is rubber obtained?

many plants. You will have seen it in dandelion and spurge leaves. But *Hevea brasiliensis*, a tree growing towards eighty feet high, produces more than any other plant. When a tree is five or six years old and about twenty feet high 'tapping' it to obtain the latex begins. Tapping means taking out a very thin diagonal strip of bark round the tree and this wound causes the latex to flow. It drips round the cut and is caught in a little clay bowl like a flower pot. Every day during the season a 'tapper' goes round his trees to collect the latex and to clean the wound for tomorrow's harvest to run easily. It is then taken to the factory and made into crude rubber and eventually sent in sheets or blocks to the factory that makes tyres or wellington boots or whatever.

are easily available in quantity the trees are continually pruned so never reach their natural height. Cloves consist of dried unopened flower buds of another tropical tree, one of the Myrtle family—to which Eucalyptus also belongs.

All of these spices are from trees which have been used in the service of man for centuries.

Is tree sap of any use to man?

The real importance of one tree has only been fully exploited in this century. This is rubber. Although the ancient Incas, Mayans and Aztecs in tropical South and Central America possessed crude rubber from one of their native trees *Hevea brasiliensis*, all they did was to make shoes, bottles and crude balls for playing games.

Where is rubber grown?

As the rubber-tree's botanical name suggests the tree is native to Brazil in the hot and steamy Amazon valley, and until the First World War most rubber still came from wild trees. Some years before, however, attempts were made to transport young Hevea trees to other tropical countries without success, sea routes were long and slow and to keep plants alive was very difficult. At last seeds from Brazil were germinated at Kew Gardens in England and the young plants shipped out in small movable greenhouses called 'Wardian cases' to what were then British colonies in tropical South East Asia. So successful was rubber-growing there that by the 1930's plantations in Malaya and the East Indies produced most of the world's rubber needs. Now, although those areas are still enormously important, Central and South America has also large rubber plantations.

Fruits or vegetables?

We talk of vegetable marrow and eat rhubarb as a pudding but botanically speaking marrows (and squashes and cucumbers) because they follow flowers must be fruits, whilst rhubarb is just a stem like celery. There is a similar confusion with the fruits of certain trees—Avocado pears, for instance, whose oily fruits we eat with pepper and salt and vinegar. This fruit, also known as Alligator pear, comes from a tree wild in Central America. Because it differs from most other fruits in having high proportions of oils and proteins it is a valuable part of the diet of some tropical natives. But it is in no way a true pear as its enormous single seed indicates. Another 'vegetable fruit' is the breadfruit which comes from a tree originally native to some South Sea Islands. Breadfruit was the reason for the voyage in which the famous 'Mutiny on the Bounty' occurred and so it has a

TROPICAL FRUITS

Dates

Bread Fruit

DRINKS MADE FROM PLANTS

Coffee

Tea

certain bizarre notoriety.

What is breadfruit? Eighteenth century travellers to the South Seas such as Captain Cook brought back to England reports of a fabulous tree whose fruit was an excellent substitute for bread. Owners of slave-run sugar plantations in the West Indies saw this as a way of feeding their slaves cheaply and an expedition was sent to collect breadfruit trees and take them to Jamaica. The ship was the 'Bounty' and its commanding officer was Lieutenant William Bligh, R.N. In 1789 the 'Bounty' left Tahiti with over a thousand breadfruit plants. Three weeks later, because of his cruel behaviour to officers and men, the famous mutiny erupted. The mutineers took over the ship and he and eighteen men were left in an open boat in the middle of the Pacific Ocean. Amazingly, they survived a voyage of over three and a half

SOME MEDICINAL PLANTS

Liquorice

Aloes

Balsam

thousand miles. Two years passed and Bligh, having reached England again, voyaged to bring breadfruit from Tahiti for a second time. This time he succeeded.

Although this hardwon fruit tree never became quite what its introducers hoped, nonetheless it has a food value. Breadfruit has yellow pulp which although it may be eaten fresh is also dried, ground and made into a sort of bread. The whole fruit is also baked or boiled or fried.

Modern Uses of Trees

Many of the ways in which trees have been of use to man are almost as old as man himself. Without them it is difficult to see how civilisation could have been developed to its present state. But in becoming more sophisticated in his cultural patterns man has found more sophisticated uses for traditional materials. The uses to which trees are put in this highly industrial and technological age are no exception to this trend. Thus just when alternative materials, like metals and plastics, are available to replace wood as building materials trees are needed in ever greater quantities for making certain chemicals and in particular for paper.

How is paper made? Originally paper was made from very different substances. The first plant product used for writing on seems to have been that made by the ancient Egyptians over four thousand years ago. They beat flat the pith from stems of a giant reed called Papyrus (from which name our word paper has come) and stuck the strips together.

Oak

Chestnut

Acacia

Some of the other uses of trees.

Subsequently other civilisations used other plant materials as paper substitutes. But it appears to have been the Chinese, towards two thousand years ago, who first made paper as we understand it by pounding rags, bark and hemp to a mush in water, and letting it dry, when the interlocking fibres made a porous paper. The possibilities of using pulped wood, however, were not successfully used until 1840 in Germany.

Since then there has been an enormous growth of the paper industry, so much so that it has caused the once vast forests of North American conifers to be at risk and it is doubtful if reforestation can keep pace. In the U.S.A. alone some 25,000,000 tons of paper and cardboard are made each year. When you consider that trees need to be at least 25–30 years old to reach a suitable size for pulping it is hardly surprising that foresters are concerned about this. There is still not nearly enough paper repulped for further use and one can imagine a whole coppice of trees felled to make one edition of a morning newspaper which is then just thrown away.

Although of the vegetative body of trees the inside wood is generally most important in some trees the bark is not wasted either. In the natural processes of growth waste products known as tannins accumulate in parts of the tree where they can do no harm, particularly in the bark and the heartwood. Tannins have here a preservative function which helps to protect the tree from decay. The effect of tannins when extracted and used upon animal skins is similar and they also make them more supple. For many centuries it has been known that tree-bark tannins had these properties and so they have been used in the preparation of leathers. The process, of course, is called 'tanning'.

Of what use to man is the bark of trees?

In temperate climates the bark of oaks and chestnuts has been much used. In other

Which trees produce most tannin?

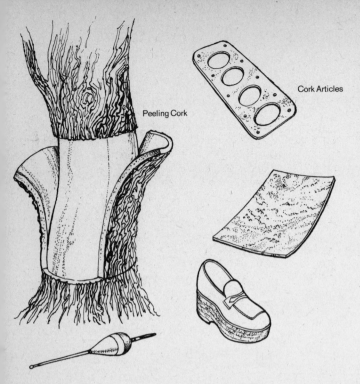

Peeling Cork

Cork Articles

like a shell off the tree. This process can be repeated every ten years or so.

Cork has a wide range of uses besides that of stoppers for wine bottles and casks; floats for fishing nets (the big dead cells of the cork hold air which makes it float), insulating tiles, linoleum and, more recently, for gaskets in engines. Although modern alternatives for all these things are now possible the natural product of the cork oak is still the best.

How else does man use trees?

It would be possible to list tree after tree throughout the world that in some local situation was of use to the inhabitants. Perhaps one example should close this chapter on trees and man, because it illustrates a once local use which has become of world wide importance. It is not unlike the story of rubber. Cinchona is the name of a group of South American tropical evergreen trees whose bark is the source of quinine, the drug which more than any other could cure malaria. Synthetic drugs are now becoming available but still much Cinchona is grown in its original habitat and also in tropical South East Asia.

It is worth mentioning here that many botanical plant names have an interest of their own. In this case a seventeenth century lady is commemorated. The Countess of Chinchon was wife to the Viceroy of Peru and when she was dangerously ill with fever a preparation made from the bark of a wild tree was given to her. She took this drug back to Spain with her where its fame grew—South Europe was at this time itself a malarial area. A hundred years later when the famous botanist Linnaeus formally named the trees which gave quinine, he called them Cinchona.

countries indigenous species have been found which can perform the same function. In North America the Hemlock spruces, which are conifers, are used. In California there is a local tree known directly as the Tan-bark Oak (although it is not a true oak), whilst in Australia many species of Acacia provide good tanning bark. These are the trees with fluffy yellow flowers the Australians call 'wattles' and which are sold as cut flowers in Britain in early spring under the name of 'Mimosa'.

Where does cork come from?

Cork is the outside bark of a single tree, the cork oak, which is native to western Mediterranean countries. Today most is produced in Portugal with Spain a close second. Many trees have a spongy or a corky bark but this tree has a better developed one than any other. A cut is made down the trunk of the cork oak (but not so far in as to damage the growing cells) and a great sheet of cork up to two inches thick can be pulled

THE TREE AS AN ECOSYSTEM

GOAT MOTH LARVA BORES INTO WOOD TO FEED

COMMON IVY

STAG BEETLE CLOSELY ASSOCIATED WITH OAK TREES

DRYAD'S SADDLE FUNGUS GROWS ON TRUNKS AND ROOTS

JAY NESTING IN OAK TREES

GREY SQUIRREL EATS ACORNS AND BY HIDING THEM PLANTS NEW SEEDLINGS

ACORNS AND OAK-GALL CAUSED BY OAK-GALL WASP DEPOSITING EGGS

GREAT SPOTTED WOODPECKER SEEKS INSECTS ON BARK

We have discussed how trees, as organisms, can breathe, feed, excrete, and live and die. But on this planet Earth few living things exist in isolation. Each is dependent for its existence upon others. Frequently the dependence is two ways; the sucker fish that travel round with certain sharks are fed with remnants of what the sharks catch; they also keep their patrons clean. Some bacteria which find a home in the roots of peas and beans make atmospheric nitrogen available for the hosts' food. Such relationships are said to be *symbiotic*. If the connection is of benefit to one side only this is *parasitism*. Many fungal diseases of plants and animals are parasites and may eventually kill their host.

Thus it is not surprising that so large an organism as a tree should have other living things associated with it. An oak, for example, will have other plants and animals living on it, in it, under it and this inter-relationship and juxtaposition of plants and animals can be considered to be an *Ecosystem*, literally a self-supporting and self-perpetuating habitat.

What animals are associated with Oak-trees?

There are two main groups: those who use the oak as a source of food—either entirely or in part—and those which use it as a home for all or some of their lives. Let us consider the oak-feeders first. The fruit of oaks, acorns, are food-rich nuts (unfortunately humans find them rather bitter although they are in no way poisonous; a rough ersatz coffee has been made of them when true coffee has not been available). Thus squirrels, voles, mice, rabbits and pheasants may utilise acorns as a major part of their autumn and winter food. In the past it was a normal part of a peasant community to take pigs to the oak forest to feed upon the fallen acorns. The small rodents will feed also upon the stems of seedling oaks.

What animals actually live on the tree?

Many birds, of course, and squirrels will be at some time a part of the Oak-tree's ecosystem, using it for protection and as a home. For a

Animals associated with an oak-tree.

Cock pheasant

Tawny Owl

Young Rabbits

Wood Pigeon

Field Mouse

bank vole

Hen Pheasant

host of smaller animals it is their whole world. These are various sorts of gall-wasps, moths, beetles and bugs. The results of the activities of one gall-wasp we all know. These are Oak-apples, which are the result of eggs of this little wasp being laid in January in the terminal buds of some of the twigs. In May the eggs hatch and the activities of the larvae—like little maggots—cause the oak cells to divide rapidly and produce a spherical gall surrounding and isolating the parasites. The galls are at first green, then turn reddish. The larvae feed, then pupate to emerge as fully-grown wasps in July. So the hard, woody oak-apples we see on leafless twigs are empty, their job done. There is a second generation of this extraordinary wasp which causes similar galls in autumn on oak-roots, but these we seldom see. Other insects cause galls to form on the leaves as well.

In England 'Oak-apple Day' used to be celebrated each year to commemorate the Restoration after the Civil War of Charles the Second to the throne in 1660. May 29th was Charles' birthday and everyone wore a sprig of oak-

What is Oak-apple Day?

apples. The oak symbol also commemorated his escape during the war after the Battle of Worcester when he hid in an Oak-tree.

Several growing parts of Oaks provide food ; young shoots may be tunnelled by the three-inch-long caterpillars of goat moths and those of the ghostswift moth tunnel into seedlings. But the foliage is the main supply. Caterpillars of several moths, such as Buff Tip, Mottled Umber and Winter Moth, eat oak leaves and can defoliate whole branches. But the worst damage is done by a Tortrix moth larva called the 'oak roller' which can eat or ruin the leaves of whole trees and seriously weaken them. The larvae of beetles which eat oak wood, although existing and originating in growing trees, are far more noticeable in oak timber which has been made into something indoors. We then call them furniture beetles.

How do other insects affect Oak-trees?

In tropical forests, in high humidity and with light at a premium, all forest trees are festooned with epiphytic plants—

Do any plants live on Oak-trees?

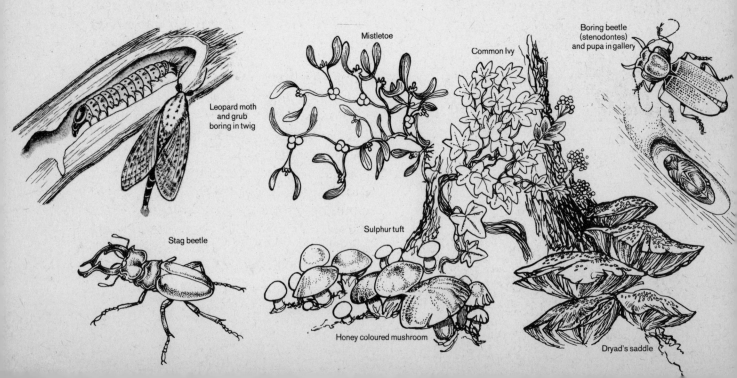

Leopard moth and grub boring in twig

Mistletoe

Common Ivy

Boring beetle (stenodontes) and pupa in gallery

Stag beetle

Sulphur tuft

Honey coloured mushroom

Dryad's saddle

orchids, ferns and so on. In temperate climates the pressure is not so great but none the less we must still realise that every niche of the ecosystem will be used by something. Thus the cracks in the bark—especially on the shaded side—will hold green algae or greyish lichens, fungus may be growing inside the timber and sending out its fruiting bodies as big white and yellow brackets —like mushrooms without stalks. Other fungi may be less dramatic but more dangerous to the tree. Oak mildew can coat all the leaves with a white mould and so damage its photosynthetic food-making abilities.

One further plant is often associated with oak-trees although it grows on many other trees for preference. This is mistletoe. Mistletoe is not a full parasite as a fungal disease is. Because it is green photosynthesis can take place and it can make some of its own food but it takes some also from the oak; it also competes for light. Such semi-parasites are rare and mistletoe is the only one commonly seen in temperate climates. Its berries are attractive to birds, in particular to the mistlethrush. And thus mistletoe could add to the range of organisms in this oak-tree ecosystem.

What lives under the tree?

It should be remembered that like many of the animals some plants obtain protection from the tree without living or feeding on it. Thus in an oak-wood we usually see a shrub layer and under that a layer of herbaceous plants. All will have to be shade tolerant, on the other hand they will be there because they have been evolutionarily adapted to exploit such an ecological niche. In English oak-woods the herbaceous layer is especially evident in spring before the shrub and tree leaves come out. Thus in February dog's-mercury comes into growth; it is succeeded by primroses and bluebells, all of which go into a semi-resting stage when the leaf canopy is at its height and it is rather dark at ground level.

Does the root layer also have its inhabitants?

It has already been suggested that the roots of a tree extend as widely as its trunk and branches; also that organic materials, the fallen leaves and so on, are broken down before their products can be reused by the tree as food. Thus the myriads of worms, bacteria and fungi all play their part and take their place in the tree's ecosystem. Many fungi in particular are directly associated with the roots and help the tree to obtain its food. Such fungi are known as *mycorrhiza*.

Finally in this section it must be emphasised that all trees, not just oaks, have their own part to play in their own habitats, and each will have its own specific plant and animal associates. A most fascinating local study is to examine a tree as an ecosystem for a whole year and to see how the seasons affect the organisms that live there.

Carpenter moth lays eggs on bark

Bark beetle burrows under bark

Goat moth larva bores into wood

Seven spot ladybird hunts on leaves and bark

Some of the insects and plants that live on an oak-tree.

Dutch Elm Disease

Tree Cutting

Forest Fire

The death of trees.

Enemies of Trees

It will be seen already in examining certain animals or fungi that in going about their normal life cycles they are harming their host-trees. However, in the wild it is most unusual for such things to develop into an epidemic which actually kills off quantities of trees. An exception to this is the Dutch Elm Disease which is currently a scourge in Britain, having done much damage in the U.S.A. This fungal disease is carried by a bark beetle and is killing huge quantities of hedgerow trees. But after all many of these organisms are host-specific—that is they can only live on one host—and it would not be in their interest to kill them. So it is usually only when man plants trees in dense stands, orchards or plantations where an easy build up of any pest or disease is possible that real damage is caused. And so often, in breeding trees with certain characteristics, resistance to insect or fungal attack is lost.

The two answers to this question must cover natural and unnatural effects. Both are linked in one word: fire. Forest fires are the most devastating and irrevocable disasters that can occur. Although forest fires have occurred since earliest times through lightning they are now much more frequently caused by the carelessness of man. Such fires are the greatest fear of foresters and summer-long watches are kept from high towers to notice the first whiff of smoke.

What causes most damage to trees?

Planting Conifer

Re-claiming waste paper

Planting trees on housing estates

What man can do.

Coniferous forests in dry seasons are particularly vulnerable. A fire sweeping through woodland drives all life before it and what cannot get away dies with the trees. Thus all members of the eco-system are affected by it and it may be years before woodland is able to regenerate. In certain situations when the tree cover is removed the once protected soil is washed away and the area is altered for ever.

Man can in many circumstances be considered an enemy of trees. **Is man an enemy of trees?** His deforestation by fire, axe or his grazing animals may, as indicated above, so reduce tree growth that soil goes with it. And when an area is stripped of trees it may be over centuries of time that with a lack of water vapour coming off from transpiring foliage even a climate can be changed. This in turn accentuates the difficulty of new tree growth. It has been suggested that much of the Sahara Desert has been so caused and that the now barren hills round the Mediterranean were once flourishing forests.

For many centuries man was not frequent enough nor demanding enough to have **Is man conscious of these dangers?** much effect upon trees. He burnt an area to cultivate simple crops, he hacked a few down to build houses. It was not until a civilisation was numerically great that troubles occurred. This is not only a modern problem; the lack of oak-trees in England when all ships were wooden-walls has been mentioned. Long before this Artaxerxes, King of Assyria, tried in 450 BC to stop the famous Cedars of Lebanon being cut down. But now, all over the world the pressures are greater than ever before.

It does not seem possible for individuals **What can I do?** to have an effect upon such world wide problems, but we should remember that every country is made up of individuals. If everyone were more conscious of the benefits that trees confer upon them they might, from a merely selfish point of view, take greater care of the campfire when picnicking or make sure that waste paper is collected for repulping, or discourage vandalism.

Much more personal is to plant trees. This would not, of course, add much to the world's supply of timber but it would affect considerably the visual environment in which we live. The moving, living, beauty of growing trees is something which we are apt to take for granted—until they are not there. But everyone is conscious of the special times; the new acid-green of unfolding leaves in the spring, the flowers of those species which are flamboyant, and the marvellous colours of autumn; all these mark indelibly the passing seasons. Trees add a feeling of maturity whether in a new housing estate or eighteenth century park. Without them in the country, farms become factories; without trees in towns a concrete jungle results, empty of all living things.

General Index

Index of Trees

Bamboo

A Dragon tree
(dracaenadraco) of Tenerife.
Can measure 45 feet in
girth. The resin it exudes is
known as dragon's blood.

Cycad calculated to be
several hundred years old,
this tree, encephalartos, is
only 8 feet high.

Boabab

An ancient oak tree
at Hampton Court. It was
probably already a well
grown tree in the reign of
Charles the First.